T

E

b

Elephant and Castle, ... school at St. George's primary and Westminster City secondary. He went on to study International Marketing at Greenwich University (formerly Thames Polytechnic) where he graduated with a BA Hons degree.

A keen sportsman from an early age he represented his schools and university in swimming, football and volleyball. He took up cycling in his early teens and formed part of the Archer R.C. Cutty Sark juniors.

His life took a change in the mid 90's when he decided to concentrate on sport as a full time activity and became a Spin Instructor. He progressed to become one of the first Professional Masters in Indoor Cycling. He is now considered a top international Indoor Cycling Master working extensively on the continent where his services are constantly being demanded to impart Master Classes and Sessions, and to train new aspiring candidates to become Spin Instructors. As a qualified Personal Trainer he has also trained many amateur cyclists and developed training programmes for cycling clubs and teams.

All this involvement in sport led him to take on a Post Graduate Course in Sports Management graduating in 2008.

He is currently training to become a Ski Mountaineering Instructor and Guide.

Being actively involved in health, fitness and wellbeing he has been developing training programmes and spinning sessions focusing on the middle aged and the elderly.

Tony is a highly regarded, proactive and inspirational person with a passion for sports, fitness and wellbeing.

Hi all,

The last two years has been a particularly strenuous and demanding period of my life. I have had to change my lifestyle completely to become a full time carer to my mother suffering from Alzheimer's disease.

This, however, has given me time to go back to my roots. I have taken a part time job as an instructor at the new sports centre built on the same spot where my old gym used to be and where I would train as a teenager. It has allowed me to reflect on my many years of working as a professional indoor cycling master, gather and restructure all my notes on training and put together this first publication, which has been a long time in the pipeline.

I would like to dedicate this book to so many people in my life but have decided to credit those who have helped me through this dark and difficult period.

To everyone at Southwark carers. Thank you Emma for your counselling and guidance. I never lost sight of the light at the end of the tunnel.

David and all the guys at Nip Nip Smart Cycling for their support and "technical" advice.

Southwark Social Services, and to Emma from the telecare department.

To all my colleagues and friends at The Castle Centre, past and present, too numerous to mention; a big hug to you all. Thank you Paul for "taking me on board".

My friend and partner, Mary Jo…thanks for always being there.

SPIN
PERFECT

BY

TONY TEMPEST

SPONSORED BY

SMART CYCLING

TABLE OF CONTENTS

Indoor Cycling Made Simple.

INTRODUCTION

Indoor cycling, x-bike, indoor spin, spin bike, cycle indoors, static cycling, pedal pump, pedal pumping, vibe, soul riding… all manner of terms to refer to one and the same thing…SPINNING. Defined as an organized activity and a form of exercise with classes focusing on endurance, strength, intervals, high intensity, and recovery using a special stationary exercise bicycle with a weighted flywheel in a classroom setting…commonly called SPINNING. Apparently the term has been registered and can only be used "under license". In fact the words "SPIN", "SPINNING" and "SPINNER" have all been trademarked and we must be careful when using them. That is why there are many other terms used to define what is basically one and the same activity. How absurd, you might think? How many people cycle and we call it cycling? Adding the "ing" to a verb merely puts that verb into action. To play… playing, to cycle… cycling, to spin… SPINNING. It´s not as if they have invented a new word. The word "Spinning" exists from ancient times, probably since the wheel was invented (3,500 BC) and the human race started making things turn, and then turn faster and faster until they began spinning round and round. Well that's how I imagine it probably all started. How on earth someone was allowed to register the word "Spinning" as applied to the exercise of "spinning" is like being allowed to register the words "running" or" walking" or "swimming" and not permitting its free use. "Oh, I think I´ll go out for a walk, but I won´t be "walking" because someone has registered that term so I´ll be "footing"". Yes, that´s what I´ll call it. Putting one foot in front of the other and displacing yourself in a given direction will have to be given another name. We humans are renowned for allowing absurd things to occur… and then making them official. Apparently you can now buy a star or a plot of land on the Moon, or Mars… and even have a title deed for it. Incredible.

I remember starting to spin when I was still a teenager at school. I´m talking about the mid to late 70´s. A friend of mine, also a keen cyclist, had an exercise bike at home that belonged to his parents. It had a speedometer on it and a simple cable wired up to the flywheel. We used to take turns on it to see how far we could go in a set time. That grew into training sessions on the "static bike" when we couldn´t go out for a ride because it was raining. Those training sessions evolved into workouts with music in the background for entertainment.

Riding a bike and going nowhere can get a little boring. Then choosing the music to set the pace (cadence) and power tracks for increased motivation. Hold on, this rings a bell (no pun intended). Does it all begin to sound familiar? Did we invent spinning? Possibly, but possibly someone was already doing that years before, ever since the static exercise bike was invented. In fact, the first patented exercise machine resembling an exercise bike was registered in 1796. That´s over 200 years ago.

Numerous different, and some very similar, exercise cycle training machines have been developed over the years and some now have complex electro-magnetic systems, digital screens, tv monitors and even Wi-Fi connections and Bluetooth interface. These can allow people to train together or compete while being located thousands of miles from each other.

There are many different types of Spinning and Indoor cycling Exercise machines. Fixed wheel and freewheel, belt driven, chain driven, front wheel flywheel, rear wheel flywheel, fixed aero type bars and multi positional bars, swinging bars, swinging chassis. These machines with swinging bars and frames try to emulate the real movement of the rider and bike as if they were riding on the road or in the mountain. Machines with caliper brake type resistance and lateral or superior friction pads. Others with belt friction resistance and more modern machines with electro-magnetic type resistance. Some with LCD displays and sensors that will monitor your heart rate and other parameters such as cadence, speed, distance, power output, watts produced, calories burnt and calculate averages and totals during and at the end of each workout. The latest trend is to install individual monitors to each machine and be able to have an internet connection allowing you to train and compete with spinners from all around the globe in real time. Each have their own particular advantages and pros, but regardless of which type of machine you are using, and whatever type of indoor cycling session you are doing, the correct positional set up and posture control is essential and common to all.

Many different training systems have also evolved and been commercialized, much in the same way as training methods differ in all sports. To name just a few, for example, Stages, Vibe, X-bike, Hot Cycling, Soul Cycling, Fusion classes …

Sessions can also vary from only working the legs to others incorporating the top half of the body, doing movements such as push-ups and other torso or upper body exercises, time-trialing or adopting a streamlined position, sitting up, working the core and so on.

Most people will start attending Spin or Indoor cycling group exercise classes without much idea of how to prepare for the class, what to bring, what level of fitness is required, clear objectives or what they expect in terms of results.

Since there are so many ways to train, exercise and workout, each with different objectives and goals, and there are all sorts of people with different physiques, ages, levels of fitness and differing expectations, that there is clearly an extensive area of discussion, doubt and even confusion about how to design and present a spin class, or for that case any group exercise class taking all these numerous variables into consideration.

There are those that advocate spinning as simply cycling indoors; ergo Indoor Cycling. That would be a correct application if we were only aiming to attract cyclists to the class. However, reality has shown that even people that don´t normally cycle, have little or no interest at all in cycling, and even those who can´t ride a bike, attend, enjoy and benefit from spin/indoor cycling sessions.

For all these reasons, and more, (which we will encounter as we continue reading) I have taken into consideration many different ways, trends, workouts, postures and positions and resumed the results of these studies, analysis, tests and examinations in this book. I hope that it will shed new light on the way some people approach and appreciate the sport and open up the blinkers that some have placed firmly over themselves.

As the ideal situation or condition does not exist, and I would go as far as to say that this reflection or consideration could be extrapolated to any area of humanity and living, I have decided to write this book in which I have concentrated on the basics of indoor cycle training which should be common to all. In addition I have also put forward my personal style and recommendations of how to work out on an indoor cycle machine. It is aimed as a guide to both instructors and users and, hopefully, presented in a way that it is easily understood and digested. To keep things simple I have avoided delving too far into technical terminology and giving overly detailed and complex explanations. However, I have tried to clarify or use "everyday/common" terms and analogies of these whenever they are used.

With over 20 years of experience in training, researching, experimenting and teaching on a static exercise cycling machine, I found that when I had finished regurgitating everything I wanted to express and include in this book I had written well over 100,000 words and included far too much detail to make this a concise and practical read. I have summarized this into a ´handy manual´, trying to focus on the most important, essential and practical aspects of Indoor Cycling with the aim of providing a guide to a complete, low impact - total body workout.

BEFORE YOU BEGIN

The purpose of this book is to guide you through your initiation, prepare you before your first class and show you how to get the most out of your Spin / Indoor Cycling experience.

To both the instructor and the client or user.

Arrive early, 10 – 15 minutes before the session begins. This allows the client to set up and start warming up. The instructor should ideally arrive a little earlier to ensure that the sound system, microphone, lighting and machines are working correctly, and, once the clients begin arriving, to check for and set up newcomers.

Bring a water bottle and a small hand towel.

Large bathing towels will only hang over the handlebars and possibly be a hazard as they can get tangled up in the flywheel (front flywheel) and/or obstruct the positional grip and vision of screens. The purpose of the towel is to mop up sweat from the body (principally the face and arms) and the machine.

Water is vital for hydration and a handy ½ litre bottle should be enough for a normal spin session. Avoid large 1,5 or 2 litre bottles. These are very large and cumbersome. A reusable cycling bottle is ideal.

Wear appropriate clothing.

Correct clothing such as cycling culottes and cycling shoes are recommended. Any suitable sweat wicking top can be used. Cycling or weight training gloves are also a good idea as sweaty palms can affect the grip on the bars. Dressing in layers is always recommended since you can take them off or put them on depending on how hot or cold you feel. This is recommended for people who are more sensitive to temperature changes.

Spin studios can generally feel quite cold when you first enter. Most are isolated, air-conditioned and soundproofed areas. This is due to the amount of heat and noise levels generated during a session.

The use of compression clothing is recommended. These are generally tight fitting garments designed specifically for the activity in question. For indoor activities they are especially useful as they are efficient at wicking away the sweat.

Although they are designed to increase the blood flow to the specific areas, improve performance and shorten recovery times, the evidence confirming this is not entirely conclusive. However they have become very popular and for cycling in particular, whether it be outdoors or indoors, there are great benefits in comfort to be had from wearing them.

Gloves add grip and comfort to the hands.

Padded section inside the cycling shorts, or culottes, adds comfort when riding in the saddle.

Another option is to add a padded / gel cover to the saddle for extra comfort.

Cycling shoes are also recommended as they are designed specifically for this purpose. The sole is rigid and this distributes the force of the pedal against the sole along the length of the shoe. Attaching cleats to the cycling shoes will enable you to use the cleat side of the pedal as we will see in the "Clipping In" section. They will help improve your pedaling technique and add to the degree of comfort.

You can use trainers or other gym appropriate footwear but these normally have softer soles and transmit the force of the pedal directly to the ball of the foot. With this type of footwear you will use the caged side of the pedal and the strap to secure the foot in the correct position. Remember to keep the shoe laces out of the way so that they cannot become entangled with the pedals and cranks.

Do not use wide bottomed/bell bottomed leggings as these can become entangled with the pedals and cranks being a real danger and a potential hazard causing an injury.

All these items are available from your local bike shop, sports stores and online.

Important note to instructors and participants "Before You Begin".

There is a common widespread fear of Spinning and Indoor Cycling. Most people seem to think that it is only for keen cyclists and people who are already fit, but in reality it is apt for everyone and of all ages. As long as you are generally healthy and there is no medical reason or condition impeding or advising against doing exercise, then there is no reason why you can't participate in a Spin or Indoor Cycling session.

Understand that the intensity of the workout basically depends on each person and how far they want to push themselves. The instructor may be very motivating and enthusiastic, the music may be intense and stimulating, and you may be drawn in by the charged up atmosphere and get carried away pushing yourself way beyond what your body is physically prepared for.

As the instructor, you must watch and observe all the participants of the class. You will explain clearly the objectives of each session at the start and guide the class through the session so that each participant can achieve those goals at their own level. Not every one is feeling the same way every day and not every one will be able to push themselves in the same way. Many factors come into play to determine a person's physical and emotional state at any given moment. The Instructor must have the ability to coax the maximum out of each participant and steer the group through the session.

HEALTH AND SAFETY

As the Instructor you should also view yourself as the "Personal Trainer" of the class.

Always ask if there is someone new to Spinning / Indoor-cycling before you begin each session. Even if no one sticks their hand up or makes themselves known to you and/or informs you that they are new to the activity, always look around and check for new faces or for anyone that has not set themselves up correctly. Even regular users can adopt bad habits, postures or positions that require your attention and correction.

As a suggestion to all gyms and fitness centres, ideally the instructor should have been informed as to new clients or user to the class by the Fitness Manager or by the Reception Team. A note on the class list would also be a good idea. Ideally there should be an induction session where everybody new to the class would be introduced to the activity and where Health and Safety measures and procedures would be explained. This would allow the instructor to carry out individual screening, health checks and bike positional set up.

- There are several objectives and benefits to any training or exercise plan but there should always be one main principal aim to any of exercise and that is that it should be INJURY FREE. This can be done by firstly screening the client / student / user to assess their physical condition and then giving them an induction into the exercise and training session. All this should be done before the person starts using the machine and attending a training session.

- Most people have ridden a bike before or will be familiar with cycling but do not assume that this is the case with everybody. I have found cases where the person does not even know which way they should be facing. Imagine the possible catastrophe and injuries that could be sustained should the person mount the machine incorrectly.

- Most machines have weight limitations so check that the user complies.

- Once the client/user has been screened and received an induction into the correct use of the machine you should proceed to setting the person up so that they adopt the correct position on the bike.

Most indoor cycling machines use a fixed rotation flywheel. This means that the flywheel and the cranks are fixed in their rotation and the flywheel will keep moving the cranks even if you stop pedaling due to the effect of inertia.

There are some machines like the Trixter X-bike that use a freewheel system, where you can stop pedalling and the flywheel will keep rotating, but these are the exception.

Fixed flywheels will carry inertia once they get rolling. You should never brake with your legs or suddenly stop pedaling as this could lead to possible injury. If you are pedaling with a high resistance, or a high cadence, a sudden stop in your revolutions will exert a lot of pressure on your legs as the pedals and cranks continue to roll under the force from the flywheel. This will specially affect the joints, possibly push you out of the saddle and even over the handlebars in extreme cases.

Always allow the bike, or in this case the flywheel, to slow itself down by exerting less pressure on the pedals or use the resistance lever or screw to increase the resistance on the flywheel, acting as a brake and therefore reduce the speed. Most machines have a quick braking system allowing the user to stop in an emergency.

Important note to the instructor: Familiarize yourself with the equipment you are using at each centre, gym or spin studio. Read the handbooks or instruction manuals and run through a "dress rehearsal" session before imparting a class. This will allow you to get to know different aspects of that spin studio, equipment, sound, lighting and climatization, and give you the opportunity to adjust and fine tune your session programming accordingly.

SETTING UP

Mounting and dismounting.

Getting on and off the exercise bike should be carried out by stepping over the frame at the lower part in the middle of the machine and straddling the bike with one leg on either side. Similar to a lady getting onto a traditional ladies bike with a frame without a top tube. Lifting the leg back and over the saddle, as we would normally do, creates a risk of impacting or hitting the person behind with our leg. As a matter of safety and precaution always mount and dismount 'through the bike'.

Positional set up.

Correct positional bike set up is of vital importance. From observing most people riding a bike on the road I have concluded that the vast majority have set themselves up incorrectly, and in almost all cases their positional set up could be improved. Correct positional set up will allow you to ride and pedal comfortably while putting you in a proper riding form. It will prevent injury and ensure that your physical efforts result in the most effective use of the energy exerted and culminate in an enjoyable and productive workout.

Precise bike fitting depends on numerous factors and measurements which would take up too much time in the spin studio scenario. Aspects such as length of the femur or thigh bone, arm, torso, inside leg measurement, crank length and other factors should be taken into consideration. Here we are trying to secure a correct and comfortable set up quickly.

16

Saddle height.

As a quick start guide stand the person beside the machine. Ask them to find the top of their hip bone and raise the saddle height to approximately that level. This is just a rough guide or a quick starting point. Secure the seat-post before mounting. Once on the saddle locate the feet on the pedals so that the heel is placed on the pedal. Pedal backwards until the cranks are at the six o´clock position. The leg should be straight with no bend at the knee. If the heel loses contact with the pedal then the saddle is too high. If there is a bend at the knee then increase the saddle height until the leg is straight. Then move the foot so that the ball of the foot is firmly placed on the pedal platform over the pedal axis. Secure both feet in the toe clips or ideally, if wearing cycling shoes, clip firmly in the cleats.

Start pedaling with the legs parallel to the cranks. To fine tune the height of the seat-post ensure that there is a slight bend at the knee when the foot is at the lowermost point of the pedaling circle, or at 6 o´clock. If the leg is straight or stretched, or the hips are rocking from side to side when completing the revolution, then lower the seat-post until you reach the correct position. If there is too much bend in the knee you will be placing too much stress on the knee and not pedaling efficiently. Raising the seat-post will be required in this case.

Saddle fore and aft.

With both feet parallel to the ground (3 o´clock and 9 o´clock see photo) ensure that the front knee is directly over the pedal when the foot is in the furthest forward position of the pedaling circle. As mentioned before the ball of the foot should be placed over the axis or spindle of the pedal and the knee directly over the pedal. Check both right and left knee. If the knee is in front of the pedal then move the saddle slightly backwards. If it is behind the pedal then bring the saddle slightly forwards. Always tighten the corresponding screw or lever ensuring the saddle is secure.

Ideally we should be able to adjust the inclination of the saddle to further fine tune our position but this is normally not possible. The gym, or sports centre should have set all the saddles to a neutral horizontal position so that you will always be able to find your set up with the same parameters or measurements whichever machine you choose or are assigned.

Always remember to tighten the corresponding screw or lever ensuring the saddle is secure.

18

Handlebar positions.

Handlebars come in a variety of shapes and forms. Even though they may vary in form they will all have a straight horizontal section which we can call position 1, a section at right angles on either side extending forwards as in road racing and bullhorn type bars, position 2, an extension of the bullhorn forwards and possibly curving upwards, position 3, and a central section extending forwards similar to the aero-bars used in time trial bikes. Let's call this position 4, although I like to call this "Rolling or Time Trial Position".

In this photo we can observe a CORRECT arm position maintaining the forearm and the hand in a straight line with a slight bend at the elbows. In this position the shoulders will be relaxed and the effort of holding the upper body will be in the abs and the core. Notice that the rider is not leaning heavily on the bars.

The handlebars should be used as a point of reference rather than a place on which to lean.

Here we see an INCORRECT position of the arms. There is a marked bend at the wrist and the elbows are locked. Blood is not allowed to flow freely to the hands and the rider is placing all the upper body weight on the bars. Unnecessary stress is put on the back, neck and shoulders while the abs and core are not being worked

Handlebar height settings.

Start by setting the handlebars at the same height as the saddle (once this has been set, i.e.; set your saddle height, fore and aft first). I always recommend a more "aggressive" position with the handlebars slightly lower than the height of the saddle. However if a person has issues with back pain, and more so lower back pain, then a more upright position is recommended (this will also apply to pregnant women). As you progress and improve, and your core is more able to hold the torso, you can gradually begin to lower the handlebars. The lower the handlebars the more you are going to work the core (abs, oblique and lumbar muscles) but if you don´t ensure that you are working the core muscles it can put unnecessary stress on the back and this should be avoided. As the instructor you should warn the client so as to avoid pain or possible injury.

Handlebar fore and aft.

As I mentioned before, handlebars vary in shape and form from one model to another. The correct position should be with the back as straight as possible (there will always be a slight curve) and keeping the abs tight (keeping them pulled in but also in tension and maintaining the core engaged) so as to hold the upper body and preventing it from leaning too heavily on the bars. Here we will work a bit with trial and error moving the bars slightly forwards or backwards until a comfortable position is acquired. Make sure that the knees do not touch the bars when you are out of the saddle. Try with different levels of resistance and varying cadences ensuring that the knees clear the handlebars even when pulling up with the legs.

The body position and angle of inclination will vary depending on which part of the bars you are holding, or which "Position" (of the aforementioned 1, 2, 3 and 4) we are in. Ensure that you are not too stretched, or extended when holding the furthest forward position. Ensure that you can maintain a comfortable posture without putting stress on the shoulders or back.

Always remember to tighten the corresponding screw or lever ensuring the handlebar is secure.

Note to the instructor:

Each person should adjust all the parameters of height, fore and aft of the saddle and handlebars to reach their positional comfort zone. Once the correct position has been attained remind each person to take note of these measurements so that they can quickly set up the next time they come in. Walk round the class and observe each person as they warm up before the session begins. Look out for bad positioning, set up and posture. Use this time to correct, adjust or even fine tune any parameters of the set up.

We may wish to adjust our bike settings as we become used to training regularly. As our core strengthens we may want to lower the handlebars or push the bars a little further forward to assume a more aerodynamic posture and work the abs even more. Always bear in mind that a more "aggressive" position may put more stress on the shoulders, back of the neck and lower back. If we feel the slightest discomfort we should re-adjust or go back to the previous setting.

Remember that very small positional adjustments can make a huge difference.

How to place yourself in the Spin studio.

I always view the participants to a Spin Class as forming part of a pack, bunch or "peloton" much in the same way as cyclist riding on club runs or in races. Newcomers and those who have never done a spin class before will usually pick a bike/machine situated towards the back or to the sides of the room. They feel less visible and more comfortable. As they progress and feel more confident they will gradually go to the middle and to the front of the bunch.

Try to use a little common sense and respect for others. If you are a large or very tall person avoid placing yourself at the front. You may obstruct the view of other participants behind you.

If you are just going into the spin studio to "do your own thing", to warm up a bit or just sitting-in to view and not follow the session, then take a bike at the back so as not to distract or stand out. Remember that there is energy in the "peloton" and this is "contagious". Avoid inducing "negative vibes".

PEDALLING AND THE PEDALLING CIRCLE

"Clipping In".

Before you start pedalling ensure that your feet are well strapped into the toe clips, or if using cycling shoes with cleats, that the cleats have "clicked" into position and are correctly seated in the pedals. Loose fitting toe clips or cleats may allow the foot to exit the pedal leading to possible injury through loss of balance and /or from an impact with the pedal usually in the area of the lower leg.

The pedals will usually have two horizontal sides. On one side there will be a toe clip (cage) and strap. Insert the foot into the cage and tighten the strap so that the foot is secure. On the other side there will be a cleat or fitting that will accept the appropriate cleat on the bottom of the cycling shoe. Most spinning machines will have the mountain bike type cleat fitting known as SPD compatible cleats. Situate the cleat by sliding the foot onto the pedal so that the lip of the cleat fits snug into the pedal cleat. Push down with heel until you hear (and feel) the "click" that denotes the cleat has "clipped in" correctly. Ensure that this is so by pulling up and ensuring that the foot does not come off the pedal. The pedal cleat tension should have been adjusted by the gym to ensure that the shoe does not exit easily.

Here are the two most common types of cleats.

The black ones on the left are the appropriate type for practically all indoor cycling and spinning machines. These are the SPD or mountain bike type of cleat.

The red ones on the right are SPD-SL or road bike type cleats.

Learn to adjust the toe clips and cleats so that foot is placed correctly on the pedal platform with the ball of the foot situated directly over the central axis of the pedal. The "toe in or toe out" position of the foot with respect to

22

the pedal will depend on each persons´ ergonomics. If you feel discomfort at the joints, usually the ankle or the knee, and even on occasions as high up as the hips, you may need to adjust the position of the foot. If you have cleats on your cycling shoes these will have to be adjusted using tools, usually an Allen key.

<u>Remember that very small positional adjustments can make a huge difference.</u>

View of the cleats disassembled (top left), and how they should look when correctly assembled (top right) and set into the sole of the cycling shoes (left)

Adjust the angle of the cleat to accommodate your "toe in" or "toe out" position of the foot. When pedalling it should feel comfortable and the foot should be in a natural position. It may take a little time and some "trial and error" until you hit the right spot. Bear in mind that the cleat can be moved forwards or backwards, sideways and angled to point to the right or left.

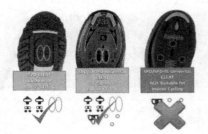

View of the different types of soles on cycling shoes and the holes and slots for the different types of cleats.

Notice that the mountain bike (MTB) type sole (on the left) has a thicker treaded sole allowing the person to walk fairly comfortably with the cleats fitted. This is because the cleats are recessed into the sole.

The middle shoe has the added bonus that it can accommodate both types of cleats. This shoe can also be used for spinning, however the type of sole does not allow for easy walking.

The shoe on the right is a road cycling shoe and is not suited for either walking or indoor cycling

"Clipping out".

To "clip out" push the heel outwards in a controlled short, sharp and quick movement.

Notice how the heel is twisted out to the side. With some practice you'll be able to do this consistently.

Try to use a quick, clean, positive outwards swivel of your heel rather than a gradual, slow movement.

With use the cleats will become worn and will need renewing. You will know that it is time to change them when you start to have difficulty "clipping out".

Pedalling Circle.

Assuming that the set up is correct and that both feet are secure and correctly placed on the pedals as previously described we can begin the pedalling circle. This is not as simple as it may appear to be. Mastering a correct pedalling technique can save energy and make each pedal stroke far more effective. Correct pedalling will allow you to produce more power at the same heart rate. Avoid excessive movement at the ankle. The foot should always push down in a flat position, sweep back throughout the lower part of the pedalling circle and finally pull up on the back stroke. Of course there will be a small positional change of the foot when climbing out of the saddle but basically we will be applying the same technique. Looking at yourself in the mirror when riding is always a good idea as you can observe yourself and correct your posture and position. When viewing yourself from the front your hip, knee and ankle should line up as you go through the pedal stroke.

Once you are happy that you are pedalling correctly and comfortably without any pain or discomfort we can start to fine tune our pedalling technique through each phase of the pedalling circle.

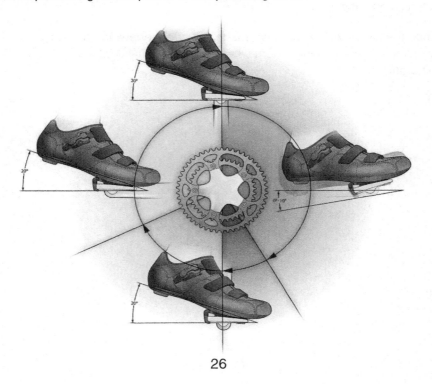

26

Phase 1 should be considered the power phase. This will take us from the top of the pedalling circle or from 12 o´clock to about 5 o´clock. As you come over the top of the circle, at 12 o´clock start dropping your heel so that the foot is flat or even slightly tilted downward as you power down the leg through 3 o´clock levelling out until you reach the 5 o´clock position.

Phase 2 will take us from about 4 o´clock to about 7 o´clock. As you sweep back through the bottom of the stroke start tilting the foot down slightly at the toes and angling the heel slightly up in preparation for the back stroke or upward stroke.

Phase 3 starts by pulling up through towards 9 o´clock. The toes will be pointing slightly down as the leg pulls up lessening the load on the pedal and assisting the other foot that is pushing down through phase 1.

Phase 4. As you approach the top of the circle the foot will start to flatten out pushing the knee forward in preparation for phase 1and a full revolution will have been completed.

Summarizing the colour zones in the diagram opposite;

POWER and PUSH DOWN through the Red Zone.

SWEEP BACK through the Blue Zone.

PULL UP through the green zone.

Remember to keep the knees, hips and pelvis stable avoiding wobbling and rocking movements. Always keep the abs and core engaged and the butt firmly and correctly placed on the saddle.

Cadence.

Cadence is defined as the number of revolutions of the crank per minute. In the section The Pedaling Circle we covered the different phases through which the foot goes while completing one full circle. However many full circles are completed in one minute will determine the Revolutions per Minute or RPM. There is a correlation between wheel speed and cadence but this can vary due to the use of gears. Indoor cycling machines do not generally have gears. They use friction to apply pressure on the flywheel increasing or reducing the level of resistance thus creating the sensation of going uphill, downhill, along a flat road or riding against the wind. Cadence is usually set by the cyclist with the aim of reducing and minimizing muscular fatigue. In studies it has been found that less pedal force is applied when pedaling at around 80-90 RPM while maintaining the same power output. The same power watt output was achieved applying less force to the pedal and therefore exerting less energy. Greater pedal force was found at lower and higher cadences. However, oxygen demand is significantly lower at lower cadences. The less oxygen required, the more economical the pedaling cadence.

There is a lot of controversy about the ideal pedaling cadence and avoiding very low or very high cadences. Studies have determined that recreational riders can maintain longer rides while pedaling at lower cadences (less than 50 RPM). This contradicts classic advice given to beginners to maintain cadences of around 90 RPM or even higher. However it does support the fact that at lower cadences oxygen demand is significantly lower therefore allowing the cyclist to continue riding for longer without the sensation of tiring.

Road cyclists will, on average, maintain cadences between 80 RPM and 110 RPM depending on the conditions of weather and terrain. On steep climbs cadences will be reduced to between 60-70 RPM, although they can go lower than 50 RPM but maintaining lower cadences can also affect balance and inertia.

Track cyclists, on the other hand, can go up to cadences of over 150 RPM. This is due to the fact that track bikes do not have gears and to achieve greater speed and "go faster" the cyclists must inevitably pedal faster. This demands a high level of muscular force and pedaling technique.

Similar to most Spin machines track bikes have a fixed wheel system forcing the cyclist to keep pedaling while the bike is moving.

BMX riders have to pedal very fast to maintain high speeds since they do not have gears, but unlike track bikes they have a freewheel system allowing them to coast when not pedaling.

However, in their short bursts of acceleration they can reach cadences over 160 RPM.

Mountain bikers will use a mix of these techniques depending on the conditions of the terrain, using high cadences allowing for rapid changes in speed and low cadences and "grinding" gear ratios to elevate the body and exert less pressure on the saddle.

So we can see that we are talking about a very wide range of cadences. Less than 50 RPM to cadences in excess of 150 RPM.

Posture and Position.

Once the saddle and handlebars have been set up you are half way to adopting the correct position on the bike. Start pedalling with a low level of resistance. We should always be in control of the flywheel when pedalling, even at low resistance levels. Remember to apply the pedalling technique as seen in the Pedalling Circle.

The automatic action to hold onto the handlebars should be avoided to begin with. Sit up with the Core in tension; i.e., "nice ´n´ tight".

The Core is a complex group of muscles that acts as a stabilizer and a force transfer centre. When we refer to the Core we are normally implying the Abdominal, Oblique and Lumbar muscle groups but it also includes deeper muscles such as the pelvic floor and the diaphragm. These encircle the centre of the torso and hold the upper or top half of the body.

Sit up without placing all your weight on the saddle. Project the body up keeping the back straight and the Core tight. Push down on the pedals to elevate the body without taking your butt off the saddle, just releasing a little pressure off the saddle. This is where you will feel if you have put enough resistance on the flywheel. If you start pedalling too fast, or feel that you are slipping forwards along the saddle, this means that you have not increased the level of resistance enough. Increase the resistance level a little until you can feel the body elevating slightly.

Pedal for a while in this upright position while instructions are given about the objectives of the session, about breathing technique and hydration.

Then place the hands on the bars. The body will have inclined forwards. The tendency is for people to lean heavily on the bars. This should be avoided.

INCORRECT position (left).

The elbows are locked, there is a marked bend at the wrists and the shoulders are pushed up.

The weight of the upper body is placed on the shoulders, back and neck causing unnecessary stress to those areas.

Leaning on the bars puts stress on the back of the neck and the shoulders.

CORRECT position (below).

A simple way to avoid this is to relax the shoulders by lowering them. A slight bend at the elbows will immediately relax the shoulders and neck placing the effort of holding the top half of the body with the core. This is a bit like holding the ´Plank´ position only not so extreme. However, we will be holding this throughout the whole session so it does require a certain amount of effort. Ideally we should be conscious of this posture continually and adopt it throughout the whole day.

Try to visualize the handlebars as a reference point or a tool to maintain our balance and to use to pull-on when generating extra energy and force in the top half of the body to help the legs push harder on the pedals. A kind of lever.

Practice changing your grip on the bike by letting go of the bars and holding the upper body with the core, tensioning the abs, and not falling forwards while you adopt the new grip on the handlebars. If your upper body suddenly feels that it´s falling towards the bars it could mean that you are not working the abs enough, or don´t have enough strength in the core to hold this position. It can also mean that you don´t have enough resistance applied to the flywheel. If you are pushing down with the legs you will be helping the core to hold the upper body. Practice the combination of pushing down with the legs and tensioning the abs to control this manoeuvre.

Handlebar design can vary between bikes/machines. Depending on the type of handlebar you can have differing places where to hold. Usually you will have a straight bar across in position 1, sometimes an advanced horizontal bar allowing for taller people with longer reach. Bars extending forward along the side allowing for a more advanced forward reaching hold, position 2, advancing to the aero bar extension part at the front and in the middle, position 3. The instructor will inform the class as to the different holds and number of each position as these may vary depending on the machine and the instructor.

Some examples of the varying designs of spin / indoor cycling bike handlebars.

Now we can start warming up.

WARMING UP

Once we have set ourselves up we can start to warm up. Set the resistance of the machine to a low level. Start pedalling slowly until you pick up a cadence of around 60 RPM (Revolutions per Minute). A revolution is a complete cycle of the crank (pedal) until it is back at its starting point.

Setting minimum resistance levels.

I have underlined this heading because I consider this to be one of the most important points to emphasize. I have included this in the ´warm up´ section because we have to establish our minimum resistance level at the start of the session. I cannot stress enough the importance of always pedalling with the feeling that you are pushing and in control of the flywheel. Even when sprinting or pedalling at high cadences never set the resistance level below that minimum level.

Likewise when we are climbing and out of the saddle a higher minimum level of resistance is required. The ´out of the saddle´ minimum resistance should at least hold your body weight as the pedal gently descends under the pressure of your weight. If the pedal descends too fast causing your body to fall to one side as if it were collapsing under your weight then you have set too little resistance. Increase the resistance until the pedals and cranks descend slowly offering a little resistance.

Once you have set these two parameters consider them as:

1 – Your minimum level of resistance for pedalling ´on the flat´ or downhill, while in the saddle, and

2 – Your minimum level of resistance for pedalling uphill or out of the saddle.

Throughout the session you will be constantly changing the level of resistance depending on the exercise being executed but always adjust the resistance so that you feel that you are pushing and in control of the flywheel. It is important to feel that you are pushing the flywheel and never feeling the inverse effect that the flywheel is dragging you. Never let the flywheel overtake you. Always feel in control and ahead of the flywheel. If you do not exert pressure onto the pedals and allow yourself to be carried by the inertia of the flywheel, you will not be working your muscle groups and, worst of all, only contributing to joint wear and possible injury, especially to the knees.

The objective of the warm up is to get the body ready and prepared for a more intense effort and to reduce the possibility of injury of muscles and joints. We will gradually stimulate the cardio vascular system by warming up muscles and increasing body temperature. The cardio vascular system essentially gets the blood flowing round, to and from all parts of our body, distributing oxygen and nutrients and eliminating waste products such as carbon dioxide.

A good warm-up will enable us to work-out better, increasing our performance and enhancing our endurance and speed capabilities. Allow at least 5-10 minutes to get the body into a good condition to start working. I do not recommend stretching before doing exercise. This is because muscle groups will be cold and stretching a cold muscle can even lead to injury. It is best to stretch when muscles are warm and at the end of each workout or ride.

The warm up also has the objective of getting our joints moving freely, in both the upper and lower body. The legs will warm up as we pedal and we will do some gentle arm swings and shoulder rolls. Note the emphasis on gentle. We are not stretching, just getting the body loosened up and ready to exercise.

As we warm up our heart rate will gradually increase. This will increase the blood flow and oxygen delivery around the body, raising our muscle and core temperature, and energising our metabolism. Increase the resistance and /or the cadence gradually while keeping the heart rate low and controlled. The beat of the music should take the warm up from about 80 to around 100 BPM (Beats per Minute).

Gradually increase the pedalling cadence to around. If you feel your heart rate increasing rapidly or already struggling to control your breathing then you probably have too much resistance applied on the machine. Adjust the resistance to a level which allows you to pedal at the desired cadence while maintaining control of your heart rate and breathing.

As you warm up pedalling will become easier so you can gradually increase the resistance while keeping to the desired cadence and controlling breathing and heart rate. The warm up will ideally take the cadence up to about 90/100 RPM. At this time we will be starting to perspire and feeling that we can begin to increase the work load.

To the instructor:

During the warm up you will have been reminding users about details referring to posture (see section on Posture and Position), pedalling (see Pedalling and the Pedalling Cycle), breathing (see Give the body Oxygen) and drinking (see Hydration). Use this moment to take a quick drink.

When working with a mixed ability group with widely differing levels of fitness remind the class that each one should work at their own intensity trying to respond to your instructions and description of Perceived Exertion or Heart Rate (for those using a Heart Rate Monitor).

It is up to the instructors' discretion whether or not to allow late participants to join the class. Only allow regular users to join the class after it has started. They will have been screened previously and will know that they have to warm up before joining the session. Discourage people from entering and joining the class once you have started.

Let´s start working.

INTO WORK MODE

Depending on the type of session design and its objectives we will adopt different positions on the bike and use varying cadences and resistance levels.

The design of the session will take into consideration the objectives set and will be divided into various sections or stages that will contain one or more of the following exercises.

<u>Setting levels of resistance during the session.</u>

Always bearing in mind that we have already set our minimum levels of resistance for (1) seated pedalling, and (2) out of the saddle pedalling, the levels of resistance applied throughout the session will depend on the objectives of each exercise and the Heart Rate (HR) zones or levels of Perceived Exertion (RPE) that we are aiming to work. The size, weight, level of fitness and general condition of each individual will determine the level of resistance they can set for each exercise. This is why working with Heart Rate Monitors or Perceived Exertion levels or even Power Metres is a good way to control the effort being realized by each individual. We will look at Heart Rate Zones and training with Heart rate Monitors further on.

<u>To the instructor:</u>

You should be able to guide the class through each exercise while observing each individual and see if they are working within the desired parameters. A quick way to identify this is through the cadence and breathing. If the person is pedalling at the right cadence then they are probably working to the set objectives. However if their cadence is lower or they are having difficulty maintaining a controlled breathing pattern then they have probably applied too much resistance.

If participants are using heart rate monitors then set the objective Heart Rate Zone for each exercise and tell the class to increase or decrease their resistance until their heart rate reaches that zone.

If your class is working under Perceived Exertion then describe what they should be feeling and observe each person so that they are pedalling at the required cadence and breathing correctly. Through observation you will be able to determine whether or not the person is working at the required level.

Steady cadence.

With a steady cadence we can focus the exercise in two directions. One will be to maintain a constant RPM with a set resistance level to work at a set heart rate (see Heart Rate Zones). The objective is to maintain a constant heart rate during a "roll". I refer to "rolling" as pedalling along a flat level surface in a "time trial" or "tucked" position. Set the scene. Imagine cycling along a flat level road that seems to disappear into the horizon. We have to set the RPM or cadence at which we will be pedalling and the resistance level will determine our heart rate. Adjust the resistance accordingly until you hit the exact heart rate at which you want to work. With this exercise we want to feel that we can maintain the "roll" for a long period of time without entering into a state of fatigue. Set RPM between 90 and 110.

The "Rolling" position. The body is projected forwards. Hold onto the extension section of the handlebars. The arms are pulling on the bars towards the body, abs are tight and the core is stabilising the upper body. Try to keep the elbows tucked in and the upper body tight. All the energy is channelled down to the legs. Push down with the heel and sweep back. The body may have a tendency to creep forwards pulling the rider towards the nose of the saddle. In this case just push back and place the butt in the correct position on the saddle and return to the pulling motion on the bars.

The steady cadence can also be used to push the heart rate up by increasing the load or level of resistance. Gradually and periodically increase the level of resistance so that the heart rate increases rising from one Heart Rate Zone to the next. The cadence will remain constant throughout. Naturally the perceived exertion will increase and as we reach threshold level between aerobic and anaerobic work greater demand will be placed on our breathing and general physical effort. This can form part of an Interval Training routine. Program recovery accordingly.

Seated Climb.

The seated climb will begin by allowing the bike to reduce your cadence to between 50 and 70 RPM while gradually increasing the resistance. When in a seated climb our grip on the bars will normally be in position 1 or 2. Here we notice how we can use the bars to generate energy through tension in the upper body and transfer that energy through the core to power down to the legs. Concentrate on keeping the foot flat on the down stroke by pushing down with the heel.

Again, we can keep the exercise at a desired Heart Rate with constant cadence and resistance level or we can increase cadence and/or resistance to achieve different training goals.

You should feel the sensation of pedalling uphill. Increasing the resistance level in relation to your steady cadence is important to simulate the effect of pushing the bike uphill. Keep the upper body as tight and stable and transfer all the energy down to the legs. Movement such as swaying the torso from side to side while you push down on the pedals may give you the impression that you are pushing harder but in reality you are just letting valuable energy escape in the sway instead off channelling all that energy to the legs.

You may have observed cyclists swaying on their bikes as they climb. This will occur on extremely hard climbs and when the cyclist has run out of gears to facilitate and maintain the cadence. In the spin studio scenario we can control our efforts and simulate conditions that will help us maintain correct body posture.

Remember to keep the core engaged the whole time and that we are helping the legs with our upper body technique.

Standing Climb.

Cyclists usually get out of the saddle to add short bursts of speed. We can see this in cycle racing when a rider jumps out of the peloton to sprint away on the flat or on a steep climb. Standing out of the saddle is also done as a stretching technique to alleviate and stretch the legs on a long ride. The standing climb implicates more muscle groups and demands a strong core to effectively transfer the power from the upper body down to the legs thus increasing the demand on the cardio-vascular system. It therefore uses more energy than a seated climb.

Apart from "Sprinting" it is the most complete exercise on a bike demanding a complete body effort.

Practicing a good standing climb technique will help you develop endurance and allow you to continue facing longer climbs when you are no longer able to produce enough power through the legs in a seated position. When standing you are incorporating your upper body weight, tension and energy to allow you to continue climbing. It increases momentum and power.

Care should be taken on standing climbs as the Heart Rate can rapidly increase, your oxygen demand will be greater and you can quickly run over your aerobic / anaerobic threshold level and into the Red Zone. With practice, applying the correct resistance and body posture, using the upper body effectively to generate energy and force by using the handlebars for leverage and engaging the core, it is possible to maintain long standing climbs.

Stabilize the body and always maintain a slight bend in the knees and the elbows. Push down with the heel and use your body weight by smoothly shifting the body slightly from one pedal to the next. Make sure the shoulder moves to the side that is pushing down on the pedal and pulling up from the handlebars. This is the "Push & Pull" technique. Keep the shoulders and neck relaxed while tensioning the abs. Ensure that you apply the technique correctly, that the abs are "nice ´n´ tight" and that the core is engaged in order to avoid injury and/or putting unnecessary stress on the back. Done correctly the standing climb becomes a "Whole Body Workout".

(Photo right)

Two cyclists on a climb. One seated and one standing. Note the correct posture of both. Shoulders relaxed, elbows bent, good grip on the bars keeping the back straight and the body projected forwards. Note the foot pulling up making full use of the pedalling circle.

Here we see a lower, more aggressive and attacking style of climbing position. This would also be the lower position of a push-up. Note that the torso is lower, in comparison to the previous image, but there is little displacement of the legs and waist. The effort and control is totally on the arms and in the abs. The shoulders remain relaxed and below the head. The arms are using the handlebars for leverage and generating energy that is transmitted down to the legs via the core. The lower back is not stressed and little movement is appreciated.

In the push-up exercise (that we will view in the chapter Myths and False Assumptions), the body would be moving between the two positions in the standing climb photos (see below).

Moving between seated and standing climb.

It is important to practice your transition from the seated position to the standing position and vice versa. Just before you elevate the body into the climbing position you will probably need to increase the resistance unless you are already pushing a resistance that is becoming difficult to maintain while seated. While pulling on the handlebars push down on the pedals keeping the pressure on as you stand up.

When returning to a seated position again maintain pressure on the pedals and use the handlebars, working the arms, to locate and place yourself gently on the saddle. Don´t drop into the saddle allowing the whole upper body weight to fall forcefully on the butt. Maintain the flow of your pedaling throughout both transitions without halting, slowing down or stopping the pedaling circle.

Standing Tall.

The objective of the Standing Tall position is to work your balance on the bike while putting as little weight on the handlebars as possible. In fact you are only touching the bars to stop you from falling forwards. Try to maintain the body straight, projecting the body up and consciously holding the upper body with the core. Transfer your body weight slightly from one pedal to the next on the down stroke while maintaining a slight bend at the knee. As always, never lock the joints. Maintain that bend throughout the pedalling circle. Perfecting the technique will allow you to totally let go of the bars and maintain the body balanced and in equilibrium while pedalling. Set the resistance to a high level since you will be placing your whole body weight on each pedal as you push down. I do not recommend this technique for beginners.

Hover and Squat.

I call this the "Quad Loading" exercise. The intention of this exercise is to isolate the quadriceps by tensioning the torso.

Make sure that the upper body is held tight by gripping hard on the bars, engaging the core and smoothly moving the body forwards off the saddle. The upper body should be kept as immobile as possible and concentrate on working the upper legs, thighs and quads. As always, keep the bend at the knees. Practice this exercise at lower controlled cadences and with a certain amount of resistance applied on the machine. This will force you to push down hard on the pedals.

The torso is immobile from the hips up. A good tip for this exercise is to locate the nose of the saddle on the Sacral region right at the bottom of the spine and maintain that position while the legs are pedalling.

Higher cadences can be handled but only once you have mastered the technique.

Sprints.

Sprinting is an excellent way of increasing your heart rate rapidly and can form part of a HIIT routine using the 20/40 method for example. A 20 second sprint followed by a 40 second recovery.

Cadences can vary, as we have discussed before, but always keep the cadence controlled and always ensure that you are pushing and in control of the flywheel. Never allow the flywheel drag you. Here we can see the importance of setting that minimum level of resistance at the beginning of the class and ensuring we never go below that level.

Again, stabilize the upper body by having a firm grip on the handlebars and keeping that core tight. Remember that you will be using the core to transfer the energy down to the legs. Pull on the bars but control the upper body lateral movement so that the energy isn´t lost in the swaying movement and all the energy gets channelled down to the legs.

Sprints can be done "in" or "out" of the saddle. Most cyclists will launch a sprint by jumping out of the saddle and use the handle bars as leverage to generate power and force in the upper body. That power will be directed to the pedals. (See sequence of photos above).

Clearing up a few issues.

MYTHS AND FALSE ASSUMPTIONS

Cycling is all about legs: FALSE

Leg strength is vitally important if you want to push the pedals, but correct cycling technique uses the whole body to generate the energy and power to move the pedals. Coordination and synchronization of your upper and lower body movements are essential. Upper body strength is equally important. Without upper body strength, core and arm strength, you won´t be able to maximize your performance in all positions and postures that form part of the complete cyclist.

Areas of controversy.

Push Ups, Jumps, Isolations, Out of control cadences, One legged cycling and other upper body exercises are all incorporated into modern day spinning or indoor cycling sessions. I have even seen "over the handlebar leaps" and complete sessions carried out without a saddle on the bike. Maybe these last two examples sound a bit extreme but I can assure you they are being done in certain spin studios.

´Purists´ (for want of a better adjective) will state that these are not natural movements or positions that you would adopt on a bicycle. You may agree or disagree with that statement, but have they really analysed all the different postures and positions which they themselves have adopted when riding. I have witnessed cyclists, and more often mountain bikers, ducking to avoid overhanging branches, placing the upper body well over the handlebars on a very steep climb and how many times have commuters ridden home without a saddle after it has been "nicked".

48

Just have a look at the pictures at the bottom of the previous page. There are Road, Track, Mountain, BMX cyclists and within each type of bike there are different disciplines. This leads to many different positions, postures, and styles of riding. What we ensure is that all these varying positions, and transitions between them, are performed applying the correct technique and therefore minimising or eliminating any risk of injury.

We are not normally aware of the positions and postures we adopt when we are cycling, but I can assure you that they are more diverse and extreme than you would think at first.

Let's try to analyse and be logical about all these positions, postures and movements.

Push Ups.

Observe cyclists as they change position on the bike. Road cycling tends to have gradual changes in surface conditions, road incline, curves and bends. Mountain bike and cyclo-cross riding has more dramatic exaggerated changes demanding faster reactions and changes in position and posture on the cyclist. On occasions the rider even has to mount and dismount on the go. When attacking a climb, launching a sprint or jumping out of the peloton in a sudden change of speed, we observe how the rider changes position on the bike causing variations in the point of balance and centre of gravity. The use of the arms and torso (upper body) are vital.

Maintaining balance and equilibrium demand constant adjustments and changes in position. The torso will be lowered, raised and moved from side to side trying to generate as much power as possible and maximise every ounce of energy. All this has to be done while synchronizing the upper and lower body movements. If coordination is lost at any moment it will almost certainly lead to a loss of control of the bike and ultimately a possible fall or crash with the corresponding consequences.

Doing push-ups while exercising on the indoor cycle machine is a way to practice and perfect this technique in a controlled and injury free environment. When doing a push-up you must be conscious of the fact that the whole body will be in movement at the same time. The upper body will be lowering the torso towards the handlebars using the arms and engaging the core throughout the movement while the legs continue their pedalling cadence. Exhale as you descend and inhale as you rise. Control and synchronize all movements and breathing. Throughout the sequence of repetitions always go down with the same leg. The push-up can be held down for 1, 2, 4 or more rotations of the pedals. This will depend on the rate of the cadence and the music, and the objective set by the instructor for that given exercise.

Jumps.

Jumps are movements that alternate between ´in the saddle´ and ´out of the saddle´ cycling within the same exercise. Jumps can be considered a kind of interval training as they promote quick elevations in heart rate and quick recoveries. They enhance cardiovascular development, body awareness, by coordinating and synchronizing upper and lower body movements, and developing core stability and leg strength. This movement in demands total body control. While push-ups lower and raise the torso towards the bars "Jumps" raise and lower the whole body. As with all exercises movements must be controlled. Again synchronizing the upper and lower body movement is essential. Since the core is the liaison between the two halves of the body, keeping it engaged is vital. This will ensure that the whole body is working in harmony. Remember to always have enough resistance applied.

Isolations.

This is another area of controversy. Freezing the upper body and putting all the emphasis of the exercise into the quads. Rather than isolations I prefer to call this ´Quad Loading´. The focus is in concentrating the energy and effort into the thighs. To do this correctly set the resistance to at least your minimum level for climbing. (See section on setting resistance levels) Tensioning the upper body and holding firmly onto the bars, preferably on the lateral sides of the bars, slide the body forwards out of the saddle. The feeling you should get is that of doing a ´Leg Press´.

"Then do it on the Leg Press machine in the gym" I hear you say.

Well, yes, you can, but you don´t get the combination of upper body control and coordination while doing it on the Leg Press. I do not recommend doing this exercise at high cadences or for sustained periods. This should be a precise and concise exercise.

Out of control cadences.

Any action or movement, during any type of activity that is made "out of control" can lead to an injury. Usually people, including instructors and experienced cyclists, consider "out of control" cadences to be pedalling at revolutions above 120 RPM. This assumption is very relative and should be analysed closely. I have seen people pedalling out of control at much lower cadences. Inexperienced cyclists usually start pedalling slowly, at around 60 RPM or even lower, and gradually build up pedalling speed as they become accustomed to cycling, gain in confidence, assume greater control of the bike, increase their strength and improve their technique. The important thing to remember is that you must always be pushing down (or pulling up) on the pedals. You must always be in control of the cranks. Once the speed of the bicycle overtakes the cadence of the cyclist (very common on descents) the action of pedalling can get out of control. The pedal no longer offers resistance to the force of the leg pushing down and the cyclist can lose control of his position and posture on the bike. In this scenario the cyclist may even start to bounce up and down on the saddle as his legs try to keep up with the speed of the bike. Here the person is clearly out of control and can cause him or herself serious injury to the knees and lower back, not to mention the catastrophic outcome of a possible fall or accident.

On an indoor cycling machine we must apply the same concept, whether the machine be fixed wheel or freewheel. Always feel that you are in control of the flywheel. Always feel that you are pushing and using the muscles to rotate the pedals, cranks and the flywheel. Never let the flywheel drag you.

Applying the correct technique, and with practice, you can achieve very high controlled cadences. Just look at track cyclists pedalling at 150 RPM or even higher.

One legged cycling.

Removing one foot from the pedal and pedalling only with the other foot is something that professional cyclist do to measure the power output individually for each leg. This is done with machines incorporating power metres such as the Stages bikes or the Keiser M3i.

Is One Legged pedalling a necessary component of a spin or indoor cycling session?

Probably not, but then, why not? As with all movements during an exercise routine make sure that the movements are carried out correctly.

To begin a One Legged Cycling exercise first stop pedalling and make sure that the cranks have stopped rotating before taking one foot out of the pedal cleat or cage. This can be done by applying the brake. Ensure that the leg that will not be pedalling is kept well out of the way of the free rotating crank and pedal. Any contact with the foot or leg will surely be very painful and possibly cause serious injury. Placing the foot on the frame in the centre of the bike is one solution. The location of the ´free´ leg will depend on the type of machine, but make sure you find a suitable place to keep the foot and leg out of the way.

I consider the risks of One Legged pedalling too high to incorporate into my sessions and far outweigh the possible benefits. However I have practiced them on a one-to-one personal training class, at Master Classes with experienced cyclist and trainers, but never in the context of a scheduled Group Cycling Session in a gym or club.

Sessions without a saddle.

On several occasions I have come across instructors who start the session with the phrase

"Take the saddle and seat post off. Today´s session will be completely Out Of The Saddle".

Wow, that is enough to get anyone´s legs trembling before we have even started. Let´s be logical about this one. There are situations when you are forced to maintain an "out of the saddle" riding position. This can happen on a steep and prolonged climb when you´ve run out of gears and putting "foot to the floor" means you are going to have to push the bike up the rest of the climb.

Imagine returning to your bike only to find that someone has stolen your saddle and seat post and you have no other option but to ride home without a place to situate your butt. It can happen, and it is good to know how to cycle in those situations.

However, I don't recommend these types of sessions for Group Exercise classes with a client mix of different levels of fitness and ability, but, if you are intent on doing them make sure you warm up well before taking the saddle and seat post off the bike and start the work-out section of the session. Always set, at least, your minimum resistance level for climbing, or out of the saddle pedalling. (See section on setting resistance levels)

Always maintain a slight bend at the knee ensuring that you are working the quads and not stressing the knee joint. (See section on Standing Climb)

You can do these sessions without going to the extreme of removing the saddle and seat post. This will allow those who tire to recover and continue the session in the saddle.

Upper body exercises.

Using the handlebars in the correct way, pulling on the bars to generate force and keeping the core engaged and the torso stable will ensure that you are working the upper body. We can, however, introduce exercises with weights, bands or simply clapping to the beat. Bear in mind that using small hand weights and bands means having to prepare extra material which will just clutter up the already reduced space between bikes in the spin studio. It is easier to introduce handclaps or other controlled arm movements such as punching into the air to add elements of work on balance and coordination. As always keep the core firmly engaged and ensure that all movements are executed with tension and energy. Elevating and keeping the arms above the shoulders works the core muscles and helps develop upper body stability. As always ensure that you are pushing down on the pedals with enough resistance to help elevate the torso in the seated position and project the body up.

Instructors´ psyche and "ad-lib".

It is true that a lot of spin and indoor cycling instructors come from the aerobics and group exercise class training sector and try to incorporate elements of those classes into the spin studio. Some don´t even cycle, have a bike or even know how to cycle. Having a certificate in Spinning, Indoor or Group Cycling is purely another discipline to add to their curriculum in order to expand the number of classes they can impart.

It is also true that a lot of instructors are purely cyclists that are not trained in fitness and /or physical education and consider indoor cycling or exercising on a static bike solely as an extension of road/mtb cycling or just as an option when you can´t ride outdoors.

Both attitudes are counter- productive to establishing and offering Spinning and Indoor Cycling as a complete body workout that has the added advantage of being considered a low-impact activity (or even no impact whatsoever).

If we follow the indications given in this "manual" all the movements carried out on the bike will be controlled and of use and purpose towards our goals of fitness and body sculpting. As we have seen from the images and pictures, cyclists adopt a wide range of positions and postures on the bike. The objective of these can be very diverse but they all have a specific purpose. We must ensure that whatever movement we carry out on the bike it does not put us at risk of injury or hurting ourselves (or others as the case may be). Control and purpose should reign in our minds at all times.

The question is - Are we simply understanding Spinning / Indoor cycling as bringing cycling indoors or are we developing another way to train and workout regardless of whether we are cyclists or not?

My perspective is to view it as a total body workout which allows much more variation of movement, positions and postures than say training on a treadmill, a rowing machine or an ARC or elliptical machine.

Give the body what it needs.

HYDRATE AND BREATHE

Hydration.

Program various points throughout the session for hydration and recovery. When the heart rate has been raised to levels of zone 3 and 4 or even possibly into the "red zone" a recovery period is required. Allow the heart rate to lower and get back to controlled breathing before you start to drink. Once you are breathing in a controlled way you can start to drink. Take a sip, allow it to go down, assimilate that sip and take a breath in between. Then take another sip and so on. It is better to drink small amounts slowly and periodically (every 5-10-15 minutes) than to down half a pint in one go and then go without drinking for a long time until you feel the need to drink. Once you get that feeling that need to drink it is warning signal that the body telling you that you are starting to get dehydrated.

Breathing / Give the Body Oxygen.

Correct, controlled breathing is the basis of all aerobic exercise. There are different techniques depending on the type of sport or discipline but in all cases breathing must be rhythmic and controlled. Breathe in and exhale smoothly and continuously. Synchronize your breathing with your pedalling cadence. As with running, rowing or swimming where the athlete will breathe in and exhale every two, three or four steps or strokes, in cycling we set our breathing to our pedalling.

Breathe in through the nose and out via the mouth is what has been taught as good breathing technique for ages. More recently using both mouth and nose simultaneously has been suggested. I personally prefer inhaling through the nose and exhaling through the mouth. Breathing in through the mouth allows us to take in more air faster than through the nose. Sometimes, because of obtrusions, it may be difficult to breathe through the nose. Basically, adopt the method that works best for you and that supplies your body with enough oxygen to allow you to control your heart rate and keep the exercise as aerobic as possible.

Once the body stops receiving sufficient oxygen the exercise will become anaerobic. Your heart rate will increase and the maximising burning effect of the exercise will be substituted by a power muscle building exercise. (See section on Aerobic / Anaerobic Exercise).

Listen to your heart.

TRAINING OUR HEART

Aerobic / Anaerobic Exercise.

Aerobic exercise will supply the body with sufficient oxygen to maintain a constant, continuous level of activity. This activity is generally considered to be light and can be maintained of long distances and periods of time. No other source of energy is required.

Anaerobic exercise will demand more oxygen than that being supplied by breathing; therefore the body will look for other sources of energy to supply the extra needs of the muscles. The muscles will begin to break down sugars which in turn will produce lactic acid as a "by-product". These exercises tend to be short, sharp burst of intense activity over short distances and short periods of time.

Both types of exercise burn fat and incorporating both types of activity, aerobic and anaerobic, into your training routine is highly recommended, but to maximize the fat burning effect it I would advise to maintain a low, controlled heart rate while carrying out a light, long duration activity.

Aerobic exercise increases your endurance and cardiac health while anaerobic exercise will help you gain lean muscle mass. Building muscle mass is important because the larger the muscle mass the more energy it will consume and consequently more burning effect. The ideal situation is to create training routines that incorporates a good balance of both types of exercise.

Exercise and train using a Heart Rate Monitor.

Using a HRM to analyse and focus your training and exercise routine is an important tool which will help you improve your fitness levels and body composition. To get the most out of your HRM you must understand how it works, what all those numbers that appear on the screen or on your watch mean and how to find your personal Heart Rate Zones. You must also understand how your body works and how it responds to working out within different HR zones. To begin using a Heart Rate Monitor we must first determine our Rest Heart Rate and our Maximum Heart Rate. With this data we can establish our Heart Rate Zones.

Heart Rate Zones.

Wearing a Heart Rate Monitor during your workout is probably one the best and (probably) cheapest tools you can use. It will allow you to monitor and control your heart rate during the exercise helping you achieve your training goals with greater precision. It is common knowledge that "fat burns at a low heart rate", but what is that heart rate and how do you determine it. The most precise way to do this is by carrying out a Stress Test, or Physiological Test, but these can be costly and have to be carried out by trained physicians in laboratory conditions. A Stress Test will determine your maximum and minimum heart rates, your threshold level between aerobic and anaerobic exercise, the level at which you start producing lactic acid and at what rate you can get rid of it.

All this sounds very complicated and scientific and is not necessary for the regular client or user of the gym or the Spin / Indoor Cycling class. When asked, the majority of people said that their reasons for attending the gym were getting fit, losing weight and to generally feel better. A small percentage said that they were aiming to complete a half marathon, or even a full marathon, or some other type of sporting event but no one ('till now) has approached me saying that their objective is to win a medal at the next Olympic games.

Bearing this in mind, working out your optimum Hear Rate Training Zones is a relatively easy task. First we must determine our Maximum Heart Rate and our Rest Heart Rate.

Rest Heart Rate.

Find out what your Rest Heart Rate is by taking your pulse first thing when you wake up and before you get out of bed. Count the number of heart beats in a minute. You can also do this by counting your heartbeats during 15 seconds and multiply by 4. The total will be practically the same. Very easy. Take a note of the number and do this during a few days to work out the average. It is best taken when you are well rested, preferably after a good nights´ sleep or after a 20 minute nap on the sofa. Illnesses and stress will vary the result so make sure these are not affecting you at the time. If you already have a Heart Rate Monitor put it on before lying down.

Take into consideration that as you get fitter your heart rate will also lower. This is because the heart is a muscle and it becomes more efficient at pumping blood around the body as you increase your fitness level. Check your resting heart rate once a month and take note of the variations.

The average Rest Heart Rate is between 60 and 70 Beats per Minute (BPM). Highly trained athletes can have Rest Heart Rates as low as 40 BPM and an unfit person may have a RHR of over 80 BPM.

Maximum Heart Rate.

Finding your Maximum Heart Rate (MHR) is a little more complicated. There are various ways to do this but I am going to whittle these down to two. The first could be considered the simplest method. Simply subtract your age from 220 and "voilà" there you have it. Nothing complicated or scientific about that. This is a very rough guide to calculating our maximum heart rate but totally recommended for those who are starting out, don´t do exercise and consider themselves to be unfit. It is an age-predicted method and does not take into consideration your fitness level or genetic factors that can make your heart beat up to +/− 20 beats per minute.

Simple method example:

The "average" 35 year old person will subtract 35 from 220. This equals 185. That is a 35 year old person´s Maximum Heart Rate.

The other way requires a bit more effort and I would recommend this one to those of you who consider yourselves to be a fit person, i.e.; you regularly cycle, run or swim, practice some kind of sport and/or work out at the gym. You will probably want to know more precisely what your maximum heart rate is.

A more precise method:

Start warming up on a treadmill or spin bike for at least 10 minutes until you start to perspire. (Follow the Warm Up method described before). Slowly increase the resistance, speed, cadence, incline (depending on which machine you are working), keeping an eye on your Heart Rate. As the intensity of the exercise increases so will the demand on your heart to pump blood around the body and your heart rate will be going up.

Increase the intensity of the exercise until you reach a point that your heart rate no longer increases, your breathing becomes uncontrolled and you feel that you cannot continue at that intensity. Take a note of your heart rate at that moment. That reading will be your Maximum Heart Rate (MHR). Then slowly start decreasing the intensity, reducing resistance and speed, and follow your heart rate as it gradually comes down while you recover. Don't stop all of a sudden. Gradually get back to controlled breathing and a lower heart rate. The whole process will take between 20 – 30 minutes.

Calculating your Heart Rate Zones.

Having established your Maximum and Rest Heart Rates we can determine your Heart Rate Reserve and start to calculate our training Heart Rate Zones.

If we look into Heart Rate studies and publications in depth we can see that it is a vast area of investigation and study with wide ranging conclusions. The majority of studies divide these into five training zones but the Association of British Cycling Coaches recommends a six-zone system. There are differing views and tables establishing different Heart Rate Zones and percentages depending on the intensity of the training session, and to complicate matters even more, with subdivisions of each of these. My intention here, as I established at the beginning of this book, is to simplify and clarify everything as much as possible.

Heart Rate Reserve.

This is the number we arrive at by subtracting our RHR from our MHR. Taking our average 35 year old person as an example, and, assuming an average RHR of 65 BPM and having established via the simple age-predicted method that the MHR was 185 BPM we arrive at a Heart Rate Reserve of 120 (185-65= 120).

Zone 1 - Very Light - 50-60% of HRR + RHR

Zone 1 can be considered as the Warm Up and Cool Down zone. The first few minutes of the work out will always be the "warm up" period and it is very important that the body is warm before we start increasing the intensity. At the end of the work out always allow a few minutes for the body to return to a calm state and never stop abruptly.

Zone 2 – Light to Moderate – 60-70% of HRR + RHR

This is the Fat –Burning zone that will build up our basic fitness and endurance while shedding those extra pounds as a bonus. It will also allow us to re-energize our muscles. To maximize training sessions within this zone make them last at least 30 - 45 minutes and, if you can afford the time, even longer.

Zone 3 – Moderate to Hard – 70-80% of HRR + RHR

This is considered the upper limit of aerobic training. Training in this zone will strengthen the heart and develop your cardiovascular system. An efficient cardio-vascular system has the ability to transport more oxygen to, and carbon dioxide away from the working muscles. You will still get some of the effect of Fat – Burning but you will notice a marked increase in your fitness and strength.

Zone 4 – Very Hard – 80-90% of HRR + RHR

Here we are entering the Anaerobic Zone. Each person will find their Anaerobic Threshold around these levels of heart rate training. The body will start producing Lactic Acid as you push yourself into exhaustive anaerobic work. Athletes work in this zone to improve performance. I do not recommend working in this zone if your objective is solely weight loss.

We hear a lot about Lactic Acid but most people know very little about it. For the vast majority of us it is not something we need worry about but I will try to outline this briefly. At lower heart rates the body burns more fat to produce the energy required to work the muscles but once we enter the anaerobic zone the body starts burning the glycogen that is stored within the muscles. It is basically a carbohydrate burning exercise. The result, or by-product, of burning glycogen is lactic acid. The body will try to remove or eliminate this lactic acid but there will be a point where it will no longer be able to get rid of it fast enough and that is where you will begin to feel that it hurts. This is the "No Pain, No Gain" type of training. You will have reached your Anaerobic Threshold (AT). Athletes train to increasing their ability to get rid of this lactic acid for longer periods of time and therefore increasing their Anaerobic Threshold.

Zone 5 – Maximum – 90-100% of HRR + RHR

I call this the Red Line Zone. You should only delve into this zone for short periods and effectively to develop speed. The goal is to go as fast as you can for as long as you can. It is exhausting and purely anaerobic. Again it is "No pain, No gain" and reserved for very High Intensity Interval Training.

Heart Rate training zones can also be calculated by applying the percentage directly from your Maximum Heart Rate but these figures do not take into consideration your Rest Heart Rate. I personally find using the HRR to be more exact and I am able to fine tune my training zones more precisely.

Beware of the average heart rate shown on the display. This does not necessarily indicate that you have been training at that rate throughout the exercise. You may have been working at much higher and lower levels as in a HIIT training session when in reality you wanted to work out constantly within one heart rate zone.

Final notes to the instructor:

Code of Conduct.

As the Instructor and the person responsible for directing the class correctly and ensuring the health and safety of all the participants I would add the following points to be adopted as standard procedure.

Make sure you arrive early, preferably 10 to 15 minutes before your clients, and have checked the spin studio sound and lighting system and that the air conditioning is working and at the correct or desirable temperature. Once all the participants are in the studio, set up and warming up and you are ready to commence the class close the studio door/s, start the sound and dim the lights or start the lighting system or projection that is going to be used.

Closing the door has several very important functions. These are usually fire resistant doors and by law should always be closed. They can only be maintained open when using an approved mechanism that will (if there is a fire) deactivate allowing the doors to close and function as they were intended. Remember that it can be considered a criminal offence to maintain a fire resistant door open forcefully by placing a chock or other object impeding the door to close.

Most sport centres and especially exercise studios have air-conditioning systems to regulate the temperature in each area. Keeping the doors open will reduce the efficiency of the cooling system and even have the reverse effect on the room temperature as the cool air escapes via the open door.

These doors also act as sound isolators. The sound (decibels) generated within an exercise studio during a session can be very loud and elevated. Maintaining the doors closed keeps the sound within the studio so as not to affect and disturb the neighbouring areas.

Keeping the doors open invites onlookers to peer in or even walk into the room. Most participants to an exercise session appreciate having some privacy and not being looked at by people from outside or not partaking in the class.

Another very good reason to keep the doors closed is to protect the exercise equipment, sound system and other items in the room from being misused, mistreated or even stolen. A person may stray into a studio and start using the equipment without knowing how to do so correctly and could even injure themselves in the process. There must always be a qualified person present to inform and supervise.

Allowing late participants to enter the session once it has started is a question of discretion that I would leave up to each individual instructor to decide. If it is a regular client, and more so if they have spoken to you beforehand and warned you that they may be late then I would consider that acceptable. Absolutely not to a person who is new to the class and has not been screened, set-up and correctly inducted beforehand.

DESIGNING THE SESSION

Elements to include in your sessions.

When designing a workout session, whether it be an Indoor Cycling, Spin or any other training exercise, it is essential to have a clear idea of what type of training session you are going to configure. Start by setting clear concise objectives and the expected results.

- Set up: Insure correct positional set up and set minimum pedalling resistance.

- Warm up: Pedalling gently for between 5 to 10 minutes gradually increasing resistance and cadence.

- Roll: Cycling along a flat continuous road maintaining constant speed / cadence. This can be a "time trial" type section or a "stroll in the park" type ride. It depends on the amount of resistance, cadence and posture on the bike.

- Climb: Higher resistance and lower cadence. In a hill climb situation you should feel as if you are pushing the bike uphill. A climb can be seated or out of the saddle.

- Seated Climb: Set enough resistance so that you feel that you have to push harder down on the pedals. Get to know your minimum resistance for climbing. You should pull on the bars towards the body and, while tightening the abs, channel the energy down to the legs.

- Standing climb: Out of the saddle and with a minimum climbing resistance set (remember that the cranks must at least hold your body weight, and as you transfer your body weight from one pedal to the other, the cranks gently and smoothly go down). As you increase resistance on the climb you should feel the need to start using the bars for leverage and implicating the upper body into helping the legs push down on the pedals.

- Sprints: Short bursts of intense energy. Ensure that you are always in control of the flywheel and that you are always pushing. Never allow the flywheel to drag your legs. Never go below that minimum level of resistance set at the beginning of the class. Cadences can be high but always controlled. (See section on Cadence). There should be no bouncing on the saddle. I would not recommend extending a sprint for more than 30 seconds.

Include:

- H.I.I.T. / L.I.I.T (see sections on High Intensity and Low Intensity Interval Training).

Variations:

- Push Ups, Jumps, Isolations, High / Low cadences, One legged cycling and other upper body exercises.

- Combinations: Roll with intermittent sprints. Rolling road up and down slight incline and short descent. Sudden change from smooth roll to sharp hard climb. Accelerations, breakaways with sudden surges and bursts/explosions of energy.

Session Profile:

- Emulate the profile of a Tour or race stage. There are plenty of profiles of races and routes of popular, famous and legendary rides and climbs available through different websites. Adapt your session to follow the profile of your chosen route.

- Ladder profile. Gradually increasing the resistance while maintaining the same cadence. Start off in the saddle and eventually move into the climbing position as resistance becomes too hard to maintain in the seated position. There are variations of the Ladder profile. You can allow for recoveries, make the session continuous endurance or add interval training.

- Pyramid profile. First half uphill then second half downhill.

- Inverted Pyramid profile. First half downhill and second half uphill.

- Time Trial Session. Continuous constant cadence along a relatively flat profile working on continuous effort with little or no recoveries.

Always remember that sessions should be adapted to the general class level. It is not the same instructing a class of newcomers or a class of highly trained and competitive cyclists. Different groups and individuals will have differing goals and objectives. Adapt your sessions to the group you are instructing.

Prepare or adapt sessions according to the equipment you will be using at each centre. That is why, as I have mentioned previously, reading instruction manuals and manufacturer recommendations beforehand is essential. Know what equipment and set-up you have at your disposal at each centre beforehand to avoid possible / probable surprises or disappointments.

COOL-DOWN AND STRETCHING

I have included the "Cool-Down and Stretching" in the "Designing the Session" section as I consider it to be an integral part of any workout. However it receives a bold title to emphasise its importance.

Cooling Down.

Consider the Cool Down and the Stretching sections as an integral and equally important part of the session. Once we have completed the exercise section of the session we will immediately start the "cool down".

Do not stop pedalling all of a sudden. It is very important to approach the cool down as an inverse warm up. We will gradually lower our heart rate, which probably went into the Maximum Heart Rate Zone in the final moments of the session, and get back to controlled breathing while we continue pedalling.

Do not forget to keep control of the flywheel at all times and to keep pushing down on the pedals, only at a lower resistance or cadence. If we were to stop suddenly people could experience dizziness or a feeling of becoming faint especially, those with low blood pressure or those who are not accustomed to doing exercise. Watch out for beginners with high eagerness and wanting to give it 150%.

Just because we have finished the higher intensity part of the class doesn't mean that we forget to keep control of our posture on the bike, our breathing and our pedalling. The session is not over yet.

As part of the cool down we will include hydration. It is very important to hydrate, not only during, but also after doing exercise. Again we must address hydration in a controlled and orderly way. Don't down half a pint in one go. Start taking small sips but only once you have lowered your heart rate and are breathing normally. Taking small sips doesn't mean drinking less. It means drinking the amount of liquid the body needs in a way that it can be best absorbed.

To the Instructor:

Allow at least a couple of minutes for the participants of the class to cool down and hydrate. During this time go round the class and check up on each participant. Make sure that the person is recovering well and feeling good. Take the opportunity to make one-on-one individual observations pointing out areas where the person can correct or improve their technique and also to congratulate those who are working well. Consider this part of the personal training aspect of the session.

Stretching.

As an integral part of the indoor cycling session I highly recommend incorporating a stretching routine to be carried out immediately after the cooling down period. It is an excellent way to ensure that the different muscle groups that have been exercised and worked throughout the session can recover their elasticity and length. During exercise muscles contract and shorten providing power and stability. After a long or intense effort muscles will begin to ache and even "cramp up" impeding further motion and losing their ability to perform. To avoid this it is vitally important to stretch and to stretch correctly by applying the appropriate technique.

There are differing, and controversial, theories on stretching techniques, but again, here I will endeavour to simplify and clarify these and offer a straight forward approach to the matter.

To begin, always stretch at the end of an exercise when the body is warm and the muscles can be elongated without risk of injury. Never stretch a cold muscle since the risk of injury is high and can even have the adverse reflex effect of contracting and shortening the muscle.

Types of stretching techniques that have evolved over the years include Ballistic stretching, Static stretching and Dynamic stretching. There is a more advanced type of stretching, or flexibility training called PNF (Proprioceptive Neuromuscular Facilitation) that was originally developed as a form of rehabilitation.

Ballistic stretching is the "old school" type of stretching that most of us were shown at school where we would stretch muscles to their limit and then add a few bounces to further the stretch even more. The risk of injury is high and the bounces are counterproductive in that they can induce a reflex tensioning of the muscles creating the adverse effect.

Static stretching involves moving the body into a stretch position and holding that position for a given length of time allowing the muscles to elongate and become more flexible. 20 to 30 seconds is sufficient time for the stretch to fulfil its objective.

Dynamic stretching gently pushes the muscles and joints to their limits of motion and range through rhythmic movement.

PNF stretching is usually carried out with a partner or a trainer and involves both the stretching and contraction of the specific muscle group.

Within the time constraint of the Group Exercise Class it can be difficult to fit in a stretching routine. It is not necessary to carry out a complete routine to stretch every muscle.

We can devise a short routine concentrating on the areas we have worked more such as the lower extremities:

Calves, Hamstrings, Hip Flexors in the pelvis and Quadriceps in the front of the thighs.

Also include upper body stretching:

Shoulders, Neck, Lumbar muscles in the lower back and the arms, Forearms and Triceps. Remember that we have been incorporating the upper body in our training session. These stretches are very important and beneficial to maintain good health and mobility.

The objective of the stretch is to maintain the muscles flexible, strong, and healthy. Cycling has a tendency in tighten and shorten the hamstrings in the back of the thigh. That can make it harder to extend your leg or straighten your knee all the way. A hamstring stretch will keep the muscles in the back of your thigh flexible. We need that flexibility to maintain a range of motion in the joints.

What happens if we don´t stretch?

Well, the muscles will shorten and become tight and their ability to perform when called for during an activity will lessen. The final result of not stretching will be weak and damaged muscles that won´t be able to extend fully with the consequential risk of "pulled muscles", joint pain and sprains.

Important points to remember when stretching:

- Always warm up before you stretch. Ideally stretch after the exercise or training routine and while the muscles are still warm.

- You should feel tension during a stretch, but you should not feel pain.

- Hold a stretch for 20 - 30 seconds.

- Don't bounce or rebound from the maximum stretch position.

- Carry out symmetrical stretches covering both sides of the body.

- Breathe freely. Don´t hold your breath.

Never stretch areas where you have a bone fracture, a sprained or acutely strained muscle. It may sound obvious but I have seen it done. Always carry out a complete rehabilitation before returning to full exercising and stretching. Inform your instructors and ask them for advice if in doubt.

MAXIMIZE YOUR TRAINING SESSIONS

How to get the most out of your training sessions.

As aspiring athletes we not only want to be fit but we also want to be able to perform. But not everyone has the same specific objectives and not everybody sees themselves as an athlete trying to emulate their sporting idols. Bear in mind that our sporting idols are professionals dedicated exclusively to their sport. They take their bodies to extremes with the sole aim of winning. These extremes are not always healthy or recommended practices if we are looking for a balanced wellbeing for our bodies. The vast majority of gym and sporting facility users or members have professions that have nothing to do with a healthy way of life. People try to combine (or juggle) professional careers with family life and other obligations. Apart from the stress and pressures of the normal daily routine, other variables such as shift-work and travel complicate our agenda even more. Finding time to go to the gym and exercising becomes increasingly difficult.

Making good use of our time at the gym is essential when that time is reduced to the bare minimum. Can we fit our exercise and training routines around our family and work life, and in the process get rid of those extra pounds while allowing ourselves those culinary "indulgements" that give us so much comfort and pleasure? The simple answer is YES, WE CAN.

In the same way that we find time to do those things that we consider "an obligation", we must also put into the "obligation" equation time for ourselves. We must restructure our agendas to include a couple of hours each day for ourselves. I say "a couple of hours" because to do 1 hour of exercise we need 2 hours of the day to get to the gym, change, do our class or exercise routine, shower and get back to work or carry on with the rest of the day´s other obligations.

I see an increasing number of people not utilizing well their time at the gym. People just sitting around, doing more on their Smartphone than on the machine where they are sitting.

Training using an HR monitor is essential to maximising every part of our training. It may not turn you into a world class competitor but it will make you an infinitely better all-round athlete. Whether you are training for specific events such as a hilly 100-mile sportive or a 25-mile time trial, a 10 mile run or a marathon, a sprint triathlon or an Ironman, you can tailor your training to suit.

If you just want to lose weight, exercising in the correct zones will burn fat and you will shed excess pounds in no time.

Get to know your body. Try to understand how your body reacts and responds to certain exercises, how different foods affect your vitality and energy levels and how all this can also affect you at an emotional level.

How many times have you experienced, or seen someone, several hours into a long run or ride and getting that feeling that you, or they, just can´t continue. There is something that we have done wrong and it could be one, or an accumulation of factors.

Ask yourself;

- Did I warm up well, or did I go off too soon, or too fast, or too hard?

- Did I hydrate sufficiently and frequently enough?

- Did I refuel adequately and at the appropriate intervals?

If you have done everything correctly and still feel "wiped out" then you probably lack in endurance and stamina.

Here are some key sessions that will make you fitter, faster.

Long and Slow will make you Fit and Fast.

Although it may sound odd it is what I consider the basic starting point to Heart Rate Training. Long exercise sessions 45 to 60 minutes minimum and as many as 2 to 3 hours pedalling at a controlled cadence and keeping the heart rate in Zones 1 and 2. We will feel that it is very easy to keep going and, in a strange way, that we aren´t really exerting ourselves, but we **are** exercising. Here is where we will be maximising our calorie burning. Remember that fat burns at a low heart rate. The body needs oxygen to burn those calories and the more intense the exercise the less aerobic it becomes. If we push very hard the exercise will become anaerobic and the

73

objective of this training session will be lost. Training in these HR zones will make your body more efficient and eventually go faster at lower heart rates.

Long sessions can be very boring and tedious. You must be disciplined to keep your heart rate within these zones. Here is where strict discipline, if you are doing this alone, or inspiring motivation by the instructor comes into play.

High Intensity Interval Training.

HIIT aims to intensify our training and cram the benefits of the Long – Slow session into a 30 to 45 minute training session. In all, less than an hour. So, you are now thinking of ditching the Long–Slow training for the HIIT. Well, there is one major difference between the two types of training. Whereas in the Long–Slow session everything seemed very comfortable and easy, almost too easy, the HIIT session will hurt, really hurt. Here we will be alternating flat out sprints with recovery pedalling, hard climbs with smooth rolls along the level. 4 to 6 intense periods of about 30 seconds with 4 to 5 minutes of recovery periods in between. Our HR will be reaching Zones 4 or even 5 in the intense sprints/climbs and then recovering down through zones 3 and 2.

I always advise to build up a good base level of fitness through the Long-Slow method before moving on to HIIT. With both training and exercise methods we will be intensifying and maximising fat loss without losing muscle mass.

Low Intensity Interval Training.

For many years I have been an advocate of the Long- Slow method of training and gaining fitness. Keeping the exercise as aerobic as possible without pushing the heart rate too high and avoid going into the "Red Zone". Using the Fartlek (*) philosophy to interval training by working with ones physical sensations and just pushing the heart rate up to the point that you feel you can't push further without "wiping out" allowing you to continue with your training at a lower heart rate comfortably, and then again pushing harder when you feel that you can. No strict timing between pushing hard and recovery. No strict timing on how long each section should last. Just doing it how and when it feels right. Just doing it your way. It may seem a little unstructured but I consider that each one of us knows ourselves better than anyone else, and who better to determine when I should push hard and when I should take it easy.

Recover while you Work.

I differentiate between the terms "rest" and "recover". Learn to keep on working while you recover. By varying the intensity of the exercise we can raise and lower our Heart Rate. Using the Fartlek (*) concept of interval training allow your HR to lower while you continue the activity without stopping. Get back to breathing in a controlled way and feeling that you can continue the activity comfortably. Don´t set time limits to the interval of intense training or to the time of recovery. Simply let it feel right. Let your body tell you when to push hard and when to continue at a gentle or slower pace.

How many times have we seen someone exert themselves very hard and then suddenly stop, place their hands on their knees, drop their head between their legs and just pant heavily while they return to normal breathing and to a more or less controlled state. Avoid doing this. Lower the intensity and allow the body to recover gradually while you continue with the activity.

(*) see notes on Fartlek training p.79

LOOK AFTER YOURSELF

I.T. stands for Intelligent Training.

Yes, I know we generally interpret these initials as Information Technologies, but I prefer to use them to signify Intelligent Training. Sports Medicine and Technology has come a very long way in recent times and we now have a wealth of material and knowledge available about how to improve our physical capabilities by maximizing our training programmes and keeping healthy at the same time. Maybe these "secrets" have been known for a long time. Just take a moment to reflect on these proverbs.

"Chi va piano va sano e lontano": Literally this translates to "If you go slowly (or gently) you´ll go healthily and longer/further". Apply this to Long Slow Distance training.

"Mens sana in corpore sano": A healthy mind in a healthy body. I have adopted this as my motto. Apply this to your way of life.

Nutrition.

A good well planned exercise routine does not excuse you from looking after what you eat. What goes in reflects on your general wellbeing and how you look and feel. Just because you are burning a lot of calories doesn´t mean you can take in many more. There is a simple equation here. W+/- = CI-CB. i.e.; Weight increase or loss is equal to Calories Ingested minus Calories Burned. It´s a question of simple maths. Consume 2000 calories and burn 2001 and you will be losing weight. Burn 1999 and you will be putting on weight. Provided you are healthy and have no medical condition or health issues this will apply to everyone.

Don´t "over do it ". Take it easy.

Sometimes our enthusiasm takes over our rational thinking and we go "Over The Top" with our training. If training hard is good then we figure that training harder is better. In this case ´More can be Less´. It can lead to overtraining, fatigue and make you feel mentally and physically weak. We should plan our training and exercise sessions and allow one day a week for rest and recovery and another day for easy low heart rate exercise.

Training sessions.

Your weekly training program should include a mix of these training sessions.

- **Interval training.** 15min warm-up and then 4-6 30second sprints into HR zone 4-5 with 4-5minute recovery.

- **Long Slow Distance training.** 1hr flat ride with HR constantly in or below Zone 2.

- **Long Slow Distance mixed with Interval training.** 3-4hrs in Zone 2 with 10min burst of Zone 3-4 every hour.

- **Rest.** One day a week. I would also allow at least 12-18 hours for the body to recover between training sessions.

- **Stretching.**

Monitoring your progress.

A good practice is to monitor your progress regularly. Once a month is generally recommended. You´ll be noticing that you are getting fitter and stronger after the first few weeks of regular aerobic exercise. Your cardiovascular system is becoming more efficient and you feel that you are able to maintain a sustained effort for a longer period of time. Your breathing and your heart rate is more controlled and no longer do you feel out of control as your breathing becomes erratic and your heart rate shoots up as soon as you start to exercise. Your recovery times are shortening and you get ready for the next effort much quicker. This is generally known as aerobic improvement. You get a general feeling of wellbeing and accomplishment after each session and you wake up each morning wanting more and looking forward to the next workout. Putting this feeling into tangible figures and monitoring our progress is not as complicated as might seem at first glance.

At the beginning of this section we looked at how to measure our Rest Heart Rate and Maximum Heart Rate. Again, the use of a Heart Rate Monitor is essential. Select a training programme or routine that you know and control well. Bear in mind that we are trying to replicate the same conditions as the previous occasion that we did that training session or workout. It is easier to carry this out in the gym or exercise studio environment since the variable conditions, time of day, climate, temperature, humidity, machines, rolling surface, resistance levels will (probably/hopefully) all be the same. Monitor your heart rate through the different stages of the exercise or routine, take note and compare them to your previous month's results. You can chart your progress and improvement and as a bonus also detect any drop in performance that could be a tell-tale sign of overtraining or an underlying health issue.

Variations in Heart Rate.

Our Heart Rate can vary depending on numerous factors. Let´s assume that we are working out at the same intensity, however our heart rate has decreased from the last time we carried out the same exercise. This could be a sign that our fitness level has increased.

Same intensity at lower heart rate = fitter.

Our heart rate is higher than previously. This doesn´t necessarily mean that we are losing fitness level. It could be due to dehydration, increased temperature and/or humidity, an increase in altitude or a medical issue or condition. Ordinary biological variations can increase or decrease our day to day HR by 2-4 beats per minute. Take extra care within the Spin Studio scenario when the air conditioning system is not working correctly. That increase in temperature can affect the participants immensely. Your geographical location can also affect temperature, humidity and altitude. Altitude alone can increase HR by as much as 20% or even more.

Notes:

(*)Fartlek training:

Fartlek, means "speed play" in Swedish. This training method was developed by Swedish coach Gösta Holmér in 1937,

This is a training method that blends continuous training with interval training. Fartlek training is simply defined as mixing periods of fast pace intense exercise intermixed with periods of slower more relaxed and medium effort exercise. The variable intensity and continuous nature of the exercise places stress on both the aerobic and anaerobic systems. It differs from traditional interval training in that it is unstructured; intensity and/or speed vary as the athlete wishes. Fartlek training is generally associated with running, but can include almost any kind of exercise.

SPONSORED BY

SMART CYCLING

Tony is a World Class and Internationally recognized Professional Master in Indoor Cycling. He is also a Personal Trainer and a member of the Register of Exercise Professionals.

His services are constantly being demanded to impart Master Classes and Sessions, and to train new aspiring candidates to become Spin/Indoor Cycling Instructors.

As a qualified Personal Trainer he has trained many cyclists and tri-athletes, preparing them for competition and developing training programmes for cycling clubs and teams.

This book focuses on the most important, essential and practical aspects of Indoor Cycling. It aims to be a guide for both instructors and those who attend classes with a view to providing a complete, low impact - total body workout.

Welcome to the world of Spin Perfect.

Printed in Great Britain
by Amazon

43105808R00046